# Gentle Giraffes

GROWING UP WILD

Madison Parker

NorwoodHouse Press

**Cataloging-in-Publication Data**

Names: Parker, Madison.
Title: Gentle giraffes / Madison Parker.
Description: Buffalo, NY : Norwood House Press, 2026. | Series: Growing up wild | Includes glossary and index.
Identifiers: ISBN 9781978574021 (pbk.) | ISBN 9781978574038 (library bound) | ISBN 9781978574045 (ebook)
Subjects: LCSH: Giraffe--Juvenile literature. | Giraffe--Infancy--Juvenile literature.
Classification: LCC QL737.U56 P375 2026 | DDC 599.638--dc23

Published in 2026 by
**Norwood House Press**
2544 Clinton Street
Buffalo, NY 14224


Designer: Rhea Magaro
Editor: Kim Thompson

Photo credits: Cover, p. 1 Kathleen Thomas-McCue/Shutterstock.com; p. 5 Jen Watson/Shutterstock.com; p. 6 Knelson20/Shutterstock.com; p. 7 Bryan Busovicki/Shutterstock.com; pp. 8, 9 Anna Kovarikova/Shutterstock.com; p. 10 georgephotocm/Shutterstock.com; p. 11 J.NATAYO/Shutterstock.com; p. 13 Robert Harding Video/Shutterstock.com; p. 14 Hadar Youavian/Shutterstock.com; p. 15 ttomasek15/Shutterstock.com; p. 17 Craig Fraser/Shutterstock.com; p. 18 Milan1983/Shutterstock.com; p. 19 Manustart/Shutterstock.com; p. 21 Henk Bogaard/Shutterstock.com



Printed in the United States of America



CPSIA compliance information: Batch #CSNHP26: For further information contact Norwood House Press at 1-800-237-9932.

# TABLE OF CONTENTS

## Gentle Giraffes

Giraffes grow up in the **wild**.

Baby giraffes are called calves.

# How Baby Giraffes Look

Giraffe calves are tall! When they are born, they are as tall as an adult man.

Baby giraffes have long necks. They have reddish-brown spots.

Baby giraffes have big eyes. They have small **horns** on their heads.

# How Baby Giraffes Sound

Baby giraffes make sounds to **communicate**. They moo when they are in danger.

As they get older, they make low sounds that humans cannot hear.

# What Baby Giraffes Eat

Baby giraffes drink their mothers' milk. When they are about four months old, they try other foods.

Giraffes are **herbivores**. They **browse** for plants to eat.

Baby giraffes eat **shoots** and tree bark. They learn to find yummy **acacia** leaves.

## Lots to Learn

Giraffes live in groups called **herds**. Baby giraffes learn from the herd. They learn to watch out for lions and other **predators**.

Calves learn to reach high leaves.

They learn to bend down to drink water.

# All Grown Up

When they are about two years old, young giraffes are **mature**. They may leave the herd to find new homes.

# Glossary

**acacia** (uh-KAY-shuh): a type of tree or shrub that grows in warm parts of the world and that has clusters of white or yellow flowers

**browse** (brouz): to eat by nibbling on a variety of twigs, leaves, and shoots

**communicate** (kuh-MYOO-ni-kate): to share information and feelings

**herbivores** (HUR-buh-vorz): animals that eat only plants

**herds** (hurdz): groups of animals that live and move together

**horns** (hornz): hard, pointed growths on an animal's head

**mature** (muh-CHOOR): fully grown or developed; adult

**predators** (PRED-uh-turz): lions and other animals that hunt animals for food

**shoots** (shootz): young, tender parts of plants, such as new stems and leaves

**wild** (wilde): natural places where no people live

# Thinking Questions

1. What are baby giraffes called?

2. How tall are baby giraffes when they are born?

3. What is a group of giraffes called?

4. What do baby giraffes eat?

5. At what age do giraffes become mature?

# Index



# About the Author

**Madison Parker** spent her childhood in the city of Chicago, Illinois. A farm girl at heart, today she lives in Wisconsin with her husband and four children on a small farm with cows, goats, chickens, and two miniature horses named Harley and David. Her favorite dessert is vanilla frozen custard with rainbow sprinkles, even in the winter.